A Deep Blue Green Song

Johanna Telander

A Deep Blue Green Song © 2023

Johanna Telander

All rights reserved.

Presentation by *BookLeaf Publishing*

Web: www.bookleafpub.com

E-mail: info@bookleafpub.com

ISBN: 9789358367324

First edition 2023

I dedicate this book to Caius and Adelina. I hope we do right by you and your generation, I hope we change course and take real action to preserve the planet for you, and may you continue that work by doing right by your kids and by doing it better than we did.

ACKNOWLEDGEMENT

I want to thank my husband and our kids, my parents, my close friends, both near and far and my many creative colleagues for kindly offering their services as proofreaders and feedback givers while working on this project.

How fortunate am I to have such an energizing and unwavering creative support system. I appreciate you all and thank you from the bottom of my heart for being a part of this 21-day adventure. Whether it be composing, writing, painting or performing, I am humbled by your steadfast belief in my ideas and the openness and acceptance in letting me be unabashedly me. And to my reader, may these poems be the beginning of an action, a prompt to something that's been waiting to be built by you.

PREFACE

In true tree-hugging spirit, I am often inspired to write when I'm out in the open air. Taking hikes is an essential part of my creative routine. I love looking for natural nooks where I can become still, concentrate and listen to the whispers of the leaves in the wind, or relax to the sound of babbling brooks nearby as I let their melodies flow over me. I'd like to believe, if I stay still long enough, I could learn to interpret the chirping languages of the feathered kingdom, decipher the meaning of the secretive rustles in the nearby shrubs, or learn to recognize the distinctive sounds of retreating paws passing me on the hidden paths of the forest. I want to believe that we humans still have a chance to re-learn to embrace our origin as a part of the sublime natural world and that there's hope for us yet to find our way back to living sustainably, with deep respect for our home, and all that it has given us and continues to offer us. I want to believe that we will stop taking the Earth for granted. In pursuit of reigniting this original connection and in hopes of awakening similar thoughts in you, dearest reader, these are my lyrics, thoughts and scribblings, largely written to find my way back to loving Earth. Our home, the blue and green reason we exist.

The Hidden Forest

It's with deep heart
I tell you honest

I'm a secret hidden forest
In my leaves I'll hide you dearest
If you choose to stay.

On my path to the endless
On my road to the timeless
On my hills and my valleys
And my nooks, brooks and crannies
I'll show you ways
To explore me
Most thoroughly

I'll let you know me
In the secret ways
The hidden forest stores
Its treasure.
Only ask, only give
For I have taken your true measure
And I've seen, and I've lived
And I'll never look away.

It is you who wanders freely
Through my forest night and day
You inhabit every corner
There you bend and twist and sway (me)

Conquer my branches,
Dig for burroughs,
It's all yours to call your own.
For in your softness I'm lost
And I'm fire.

On the path to the boundless
On the road to the fullness
On the hills and the valleys
This desire keeps building
In hidden feeling, it climbs.
Higher and higher it reaches
Until the canopies welcome the sky
But the moment must end,
Always so fleeting.

And the trees make space for the clearing
And the open air bares its empty truth.
That my sadness must make space for rain.

And though I can't keep you, should I want to
I will love you all the same.

The Price of Human Conscience

In the raving madness of the roaring waves
I scream to my heart's content
I grieve for the helpless remnants
Of the weakening human conscience.

To what end will we let ourselves drown in the
need,
To what end do we speed up time?
To what end do we feed the beast of greed?
To what end do the lies satisfy?

Check a box, save a dime
It's but the truth we override
It's but the poor who shall pay for these crimes

And nature watches from the sidelines
It won't chide its beloved, spoiled child
Though we cut, we scrape,
We pillage and plunder,
The world keeps giving - until it goes under.

The insatiable thirst will get its drink
When we've driven our mother to the brink.
And that's when we'll finally stop and think:
Should we have changed course, we'll wonder.

If the quietest screams will outlast the waves as
we shrink and sink to the depths from whence
we came,
One thought will consume us, outlasting the
others. ~~~~~~~~~

The clock keeps ticking,
We're swallowed by time.
The heart keeps beating,
So we must survive-
For the mind that keeps needing,
We paid a steep price.

Morning Dew

I am love
In the breeze so gentle
I am love
In a myriad of color
I am light, I am love.

I am love
In a cool coat of haze -
I am love
On a new summer day.

When the earliest rays come calling
And the world falls into place
In the smallest details of the morning
Such everlasting grace

In these quietest moments
Unfiltered and true
Unassuming and honest
I'll come visit you.

I am love
In this sun-kissed meadow
In the hour before dawn
In the early morning dew
I am you.

Busy

Busy is good
Busy is smart
Busy is value
It quiets the heart

Busy is purpose
Busy is task
Busy fulfills
It quiets the ask

Busy will call you
Busy will dull you
Busy unarms you
Taking a toll

Busy will drive you
Busy will grasp you
Busy will drain you
Fighting chaos with control

Busy enacts
Busy entitles
Busy forgives
Busy enables

Busy will fool you
Busy tunes out
Busy will mask
And quiet the doubt in you

It ratifies meaning
Running the wheel
Busy suspends you
From true believing.

Busy will keep you until old age
When the lack of busy
Finally so un-busy
Washes the ignorance away.

Get un-busy.

Lazy Afternoon

I'm lazing about today
Stowing my phone away
Locking all screens
Hiding all means to communicate.

I'm taking a break
The batteries were close to drained
-Anyway, anyway.
Who doesn't deserve a lazy day?

Emotions run high
The web of connectivity
Too treacherous a climb
During certain times.

I'm wasting the day
Throwing the key away
Just some stolen hours
In the sun
On the run
From it all.

What harm could it do?
Once in a cozy blue moon
Let the cup runneth over

Fill it
With a lazy afternoon.

All items can wait
The tasks and the to-dos of late
I'd rather be out by the lake
Taking in the nice view with you

I'm hugging some trees
Was needing some time to breathe
Taking in their fresh scent
Turn a new leaf
For a much improved me.

Today, I'll disconnect.

Relax, restore and reset

I'm gonna love me some earth instead.

A Melting Popsicle

Like a melting popsicle
Our sweetness is running,
Turning into a million scattered streams,
Like ambition's vague, forgotten dreams.

We will be taken apart, individually.
The lens is out of focus
The noise too great
The content is gazillion
The message, heard too late.

But art still speaks in broken whispers
Wisdom in hidden numbers.

By paint, by pen, by instrument
With heart, with soul, with true intent
We must shake awake the slumberers.
Before all sweetness is spent.

This is the fight for humankind.

Never Meant to Be

Thought you were something different
Thought you were my friend
A light, a sound, a quiet space
An achingly familiar scent
I thought you flowed right through my soul
Like a river without end
How much hurt can I keep down
To not show this disappointment?

A slap in the face
A punch in the gut
A kick in the shin
A bullet, shot
Right where it hurts the most.

An exchange without words
A different feel
And suddenly
What it all was
I see was not

What it was
Was not at all
What it was
To you

What it was
To me
What it was
Was only what it be
If we
Felt truly madly, sweetly
kneeling
Falling, fearless, deeply
Worth lying, begging, stealing
But now I see
It wasn't worth this need for
Hard-pressed healing.

It was all misleading,
A fake, fickle infatuation,
That didn't quite take.
My mistake.

If feelings and thoughts
Made the perfect blend
I could see crystal clear
What those soul kisses
-Nothing, but near misses -
Never truly meant.

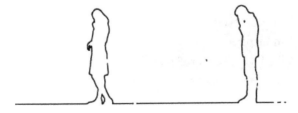

From an Artist to Her Muse

I carry you along
Like a singer has her songs
In my pocket you're the strength
That I draw mine from.
Words surface like a poem
At the thought of you
A light ignites into a prism
At the sight of you
A deep sense of belonging
At the sound of you
A different charge full of spark
In the air of you
A shiver, like an arrow, shoots
A direct bullseye
Compelling me to
Write of you
Create for you
Explain to you
Express the essence of you
The way I breathe in the world of you.

I'm possessed,
I'm inspired
Like I've discovered an entire
Universe, I'd never known prior.

From an artist to her muse
I assure you
I ask nothing, expect nothing
Want nothing, voice nothing,
Except the humblest request to simply admire.
That is truly all that I require.

And no one,
Not even you,
Will know of this earth-shattering desire.

Pendulum

Will you be the pendulum, the weight?
The fixed point to help regulate
The constant oscillation
Between these problems we keep creating?

The pushing outwards in spirals
The selling of thoughts, going viral
A new idea, some trendy name,
A movement or a slogan
Catapulting into fame.

None will be enough
We won't be enough
The time has come.
We cannot wait,
We cannot stall,
We cannot stay,
Forever circling,
Just the same.

The signals,
The warnings,
The calls,
They already came.

So can you swing the needle
Onward?
Laser focus, from the heart-
Can you be the force majeure
For us to do our part

With the power of the pendulum's weight.
It's up to you, I'm afraid,

To be the generation
To finally set things
Straight.

Born of the Forest

I'm born of the forest
This much is true
The earth comes knocking
As it calls me to

My feet keep walking
Skipping with ease from root to root
The moss feels soft on my soles
As I make my way through

The rocks seem to reach for me
And carry me higher
The trees give me balance
As my stride becomes wider
My lungs no longer hurt
As I hasten my pace
And my head clears of thought
As I let the sun bathe me.

In one deep breath
I belong
And the world bursts into A Deep Blue Green
Song

With eyes closed,
So still,
I drink in the moment,
And have my fill.

Until all worries
Bother me not

Life opens,
Untangles from its knots,

And becomes once again,
Just as it should
And just what it ought.

Musings

Do these musings I've put on paper,
These scribblings of thoughts and things
Do the details I chose to remember,
Live beyond the drying ink?

Could they travel on more adventures
Reborn anew in some ways,
When another person reads them,
I wonder,
How do the words resonate?

In the end, they are just sketches
Of moments full of feel.
When I've been
Profoundly struck by something
Original and real.

My rhymes are only borrowed
With music notes on loan
From the fluff of clouds above me
I relay only what I am shown

A mere vessel to the beauty
Of an ageless, timeless hum
When the clouds recede and

Out can peek
The smallest ray of sun.

With letter after letter
I greet this formless muse
I tip my pen and start to write
Of what I've been keen to view

In the language of dusk
And the soft colors of dawn,
I write for no one, for everyone,
Until the moment has come and gone,

And with a good amount of fun
And naught but the humblest of truths
I wish to see these musings live
Inside the universe of you.

At Night

The songs of our world are loudest at night,
In the rising music of the forest.

A steady beat of beginnings pulses in the air.
For THIS is a place that created life.

Through conflict, through love,
Through hardship, and hard-fought hope,
A balance is lost and then found again.

Over and over the cycle circles around,
From the here and now to the before,
Finding order from chaos
To order once more.

The rhythms of the earth,
Rumbling from our very core,
The melodies of leaves rustling in the wind,
Aching to be memorized by heart,

So we would never forget who we are,
Nor how we are meant to play our part.

If you learn the language of whispers
You will understand.

It's time to stay still, close your eyes, listen,
and let the forest wake you.

~Early Excerpts from Kalevala the Musical
Draft

Insomniac

I lie awake
Wondering how many lambs it'll take
To drift off, slip away
To that coveted place
Of invisible mirrors.

I rest my eyes,
Turning myself from side to side
Twitching in an in between
Of unsettling uncertainties.

What I so badly wish to see,
Behind heavy-lidded curtains -
Is something like a memory
Slipping just out of reach.

Like the starry night
The everlasting twinkling lights,
These bouncing rhymes
Intimate, evasive and distant
All at the same time
Will not seize, will not leave me be.

I'd like to earn a small reprieve
From this carousel of melodies

Like subtitles on silver screens
Haunted by the constant chatter
Of unspoken words.

What I wouldn't do
For the Sandman's lucky loot,
Madness guaranteed
In this pursuit
Of uncaught dreams.

How are the stars getting louder
When all else goes quiet?

The witching hour this must be.

Pressing Pause

A glassy surface greets
My fearless,
Adventuring feet
With its tingling welcome.

Caressing the tips of my toes
With a sensation of coldest cold,
I receive this silky, weightless gift,
Like a hug, whole-heartedly.

Wading through the shallow waves,
My worries slowly become moot.

I float.

As if in midair,
In suspense,
In stolen time,

I wait.

Until the art of unwinding
Finds me.

Until the train of my thoughts,
Like ripples around me scatters.

Until pressing pause,
Such a daring, dangerous thing,
Becomes as easy as breathing.
And all that matters.

A Room Full of People

In a room full of people,
Animated and grand,
I'm happily at ease
Babbling, laughing
Relishing in the energy
Of golden friendships.

I cherish the connectivity.
So I can't quite understand
The trouble it sometimes causes me
For the conversations to land.

Try I may
To concentrate
On the faces, voices,
Expressive smiles,

In an instant, I'm flying.
In one breath,
Awake and asleep,
Traveling to places unseen:
Forests, beautiful, lush and green.

I chide myself
And snap.

Forcing my way back
Out of this dejavu-like dream.

Yet the scent of pine has followed me
And while I'm chatting, making merry,

Somewhere deep inside my soul
I'm still picking forest berries.

The Gray World

In the Gray world
There's a shadowland
Where the sun feels like a distant friend.
A far away memory, no longer relevant.

In the Gray world,
There's a shadowland,
A watercolor painting,
The colors long fading
A splash of crumpled paper
Of one last sunset.

In the Gray world,
There's a shadowland
Where like a heavy blanket
A stiffness
A numbness
An aching menace
Nests in the marshes.

In the Gray world,
There's a shadowland,
Where the Sleepless
Live in Sadness.
A Relentless, Constant presence

Lurks like an empty promise
No one wants to make.

In our Green world,
There's a fantasy land
Of Beauty and Plenty
Where the Fortunate,
In an endless parade
Of ornate masquerades
Have developed a taste
For squandering tomorrows.

In a future world,
There's a looming land of misty white.
The colors yet changing,
Fate, undecided.

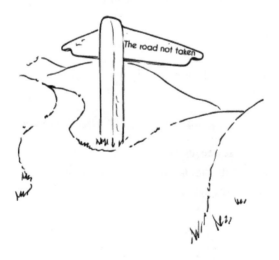

Dandelion Mission

When I was a little girl,

I believed in Dandelion wishes,
Turning to Fairy dust,
Turning to the Wind's whispers,
Full of silver Magic.

As the clouds shaped above me
They formed a promise
Of happy tomorrows.

Through the filtered light of a youthful eye
I watched the world dance in love.

As a mother,

I tell my girl to believe in her wishes,
Fortify her hopes,
Visualize her goals,

As she squeezes her eyes shut
And sends the dandelion fuzz into the
whispering wind,

I tell her to look for the fairy dust
In the kindness of others,

I ask her to create the silver magic,
And to dance in the world, with love.

I tell her the clouds will shape to her movement,
And she can tilt them, however she wishes.

And as I gaze into the light of her youthful eyes,
I fully believe in her Dandelion mission.

Inklings

Inklings and Glimpses
Frictions and frissons,
A handful of almosts-
That never caught.
Didn't last long, didn't travel far,
And like an imprint in the sand,
Stood for nothing at all.

Yet in the odd moment
I long to relive
A little bit of that "what if"

Two sailboats passing
Never the chance
But my heart still dances
All the same.

A glowing warmth
In a fleeting smile
A little sparkle in the eye
A breath, caught
A mere passing thought
Yet one I can't help, but
-When caught off guard-
Sometimes entertain.

Reflections of a Flower Vase

Why did I trust you with my care
My roots dry, my branches bare
My bristles. breaking
My flimsy limbs, shaking
Reaching for the sky
Like a last lifeline
For the smallest drink of sunlight.
Suffocating
In this crowded, noisy atmosphere.

In a crystal vase put on display
To blush, to embellish, to brighten a day,
My only purpose; seemingly to decorate.
When behind the splendid facade
An inner strength, unappreciated
Stoically resists the inevitable fade.

Soon I'll turn to rust
Copper flowers, falling
Every petal, flailing
Until the stem gives in.
To freedom, my heart will flutter
Full-voiced,
In a final call, rivaling
The songs of Nightingales and Starlings,

Serenading, celebrating,
The last hurrah of the setting sun
As the end of my bloom has begun.

Flightless Bird

I worry overmuch
I tirelessly care
I hug you too tightly
Though you're not yet aware-
As you let me
Ever so gracefully
Ruffle your hair
And I'm grateful
For every squeeze,
However everlasting
They may feel to you to be.

You see,
There is a part of motherhood
I can't touch, hold, control.
I can only watch
And see it unfold-
This must be love at its most powerful.

My life's purpose, wrapped in eager witness,
In seeing you unfurl and untuck
Those fuzzy soft feathers,

Your fledgling wings put to the test
Flightless bird, outgrowing our nest,

So many beautiful songs abreast,
As you figure out - what it is
That all birds do best.

Seven Wishes

There's a hill,
Near my house,
A place to shake off
My fears and doubts
In the shade of an elm
I find my calm.

A wish for every acorn I find
And choose to cherish in my palm.

There's a stream,
By the hill,
Where I can say what I will,
In the glimmer of a few tossed coins
I simply like to quiet, and sit still.

A wish for the piece of bark I see spill
Down the waterfall.

There's a field,
By the stream,
Where I wander in daydreams,
Gather flowers, from the wild
With grassy reeds
I bind them tight.

A wish
For every color of petal that I find.

There's a valley,
Near the field,
Where I at times
Go to grieve
Feeling broken, left behind.
Missing the people lost to time.

A wish for each tear I shed as I cry for them.

There's a slope
At the foot of the valley,
Where I climb in earnest, gladly
Working off the taxing tallies,
Until the stresses melt away,
Where only what I choose to place
In my heart space gets to stay.

A wish for the first lock of dancing hair lifted, as
In the breeze, I sway.

There's a view
On the top of the slope,
That nearly leaves me without speech,
A place to rekindle new-found hope,
In its magnificent wisdom,
I learn to breathe.

One wish for the cotton candy clouds,
Gliding by, so peacefully.

When I turn to go,
Passing the valley,
The field, the slope
The hill and the stream,
My heart, first so heavy of hurt,
Gradually rebuilds,
Becomes carefree.
And with every step that I tread
I can feel a lightness spread,

Seven wishes for the journey,
Seven wishes for the beauty,
Seven wishes for each temple,

As I make my way home.

Printed in the USA
CPSIA information can be obtained
at www.ICGtesting.com
LVHW010719181223
766713LV00045B/907